THE BRITISH CENSUS

Simon Smith

1					
Name of the Institution *Buckingham Palace*					
NAMES of each Person who abode therein on the Night of Sunday, June 6th.	Age of Males.	Age of Females.	OCCUPATION. if any.	Whether Born in same County.	Where Born Whether Born in Scotland, Ireland, or Foreign Parts.
The Queen		20	✓	✓	
H.R.H. Prince Albert	20		✓	✗	F
The Princess Royal		3 mnths	✓	✓	
Earl of Aboyne	45		Lord in Waiting	N	
George Tho.s Keppel	40		Groom in Waiting	✓	
Edward Pretorius	30		Secretary to H.R.H. Prince Albert		F
Thomas Batchelor	55		Page of the Back stairs	N	
Augustus Fred.k Gerding	40		Page of the Back stairs		F
William Peel	20		Page of the Presence	N	
George Wakeley	50		Queen's Messenger	N	
Thomas Hill	40		Queen's Messenger	N	
Isaac Cart	30		Valet		F
Andrew Dehler	30		Valet to H.R.H. Prince Albert		F
Thomas Cooper	25		Valet	N	
Charles Woolger	30		Valet	N	
James Woods	30		Valet	N	
Joseph Martin	35		Cabinet Maker	N	
Charles Benda	20		Jaeger to H.R.H. Prince Albert		F

SHIRE PUBLICATIONS

Bloomsbury Publishing Plc

Kemp House, Chawley Park, Cumnor Hill, Oxford OX2 9PH, UK

29 Earlsfort Terrace, Dubin 2, Ireland

1385 Broadway, 5th Floor, New York,

NY 10018, USA

E-mail: shire@bloomsbury.com

www.shirebooks.co.uk

SHIRE is a trademark of Osprey Publishing Ltd

First published in Great Britain in 2021

© Simon Smith, 2021

A catalogue record for this book is available from the British Library.

ISBN: PB 978 1 78442 457 2

eBook 978 1 78442 454 1

ePDF 978 1 78442 455 8

XML 978 1 78442 453 4

21 22 23 24 25   10 9 8 7 6 5 4 3 2 1

Typeset by PDQ Digital Media Solutions, Bungay, UK.

Printed and bound in India by Replika Press Private Ltd.

MIX
Paper from responsible sources
FSC
www.fsc.org   FSC® C016779

Shire Publications supports the Woodland Trust, the UK's leading woodland conservation charity.

COVER IMAGE

Front cover: Administrative staff compile information from the 1931 census (see page 50) (Fox Photos/Getty Images). Back cover: Column headings from the 1841 census form. (Matt Cardy/Getty Images).

TITLE PAGE IMAGE

The 1841 Census return for Buckingham Palace. Queen Victoria and Prince Albert are listed as 20 years old (their ages having been rounded down [see page 28]).

CONTENTS PAGE IMAGE

Watling Street Road Workhouse, Preston. Workhouses were harsh and would be a last resort for the poor (see page 12), despite their sometimes opulent exteriors. Census returns helped to formulate government policy on such issues as management of the poor and infirm, and many Victorian census returns show the destitute as resident in workhouses such as this.

ACKNOWLEDGEMENTS

I am most grateful to James Harrison, Archivist at Brighton College, for his help with sourcing many of the photographs for this book. Images are acknowledged as follows:

© The Trustees of the British Museum, released as CC BY-NC-SA 4.0, page 16; Biblioteca Europea di Informazione e Cultura/Public Domain, page 13; Birmingham Museums Trust/Public Domain, pages 21, 29 (right); Bonnefanten Museum/Public Domain, page 5; British Library/Public Domain, page 24, 33 (top); Ceredigion1905/CC BY-SA 4.0, page 41; Colonel Warden/CC BY-SA 3.0, page 48 (top); DeVo787/CC BY-SA 3.0, page 59; Francis Franklin/CC BY-SA 4.0, page 3; Getty Images, pages 1, 6, 8 (bottom), 14, 22 (top), 27, 29 (left), 36, 37, 48 (bottom), 49, 50 (both), 51 (right), 52, 53, 55, 57, 58; Istockphoto, page 40 (both); Jan van der Crabben/CC BY-SA 2.0, page 42; Jarry1250/CC BY-SA 3.0, page 12; John E Vigar/CC BY 2.0, page 8 (top); Johnny Cyprus/CC BY-SA 3.0, page 44; Mary Evans, pages 26, 30–31, 46, 47; Nick Cooper/CC BY-SA 2.5, page 43; Public Domain, pages 19, 32 (bottom), 51 (left); Sebb/Public Domain, page 38; Thomas Fisher Rare Book collection/Public Domain, page 7; Tony Grist/CC0 1.0, page 17; Topfoto, page 28; Wellcome Images/CC BY 4.0, pages 9, 10, 15, 20, 32 (top), 33 (bottom), 39; Yale Center for British Art/Paul Mellon Collection, pages 22 (bottom), 23.

CONTENTS

THE BIBLE, DOMESDAY AND PARISHES

THE WORD 'CENSUS' comes from the Latin *censere*: to estimate, assess. For many, the earliest mention of a census dates back to a chilly December afternoon attending a carol service in a church or school hall. The reading recounting the birth of Jesus begins, 'A decree went out from Caesar Augustus that all the world should be taxed.' These opening words of the second chapter of St Luke's Gospel are made clearer in later translations: the 'world' was the Roman world, which extended to Palestine in the first century AD, and 'taxed' meant registered or counted.

Such a public declaration of personal circumstances would have aroused suspicion then, as it did through successive generations, as citizens have feared underhand motives for such a head count. Exactly who was being assessed and for what purpose in that gospel story where Joseph and the heavily pregnant Mary travelled to Bethlehem is not entirely clear. The actual population of the Roman Empire probably numbered between 5 and 12 million, depending on whether only the men were counted, or women and children too.

This is not the first reference to counting people in the Bible. At the start of the aptly named Book of Numbers, God tells Moses to count those Israelites in the desert who are capable of bearing arms and are fit for military duty (there were 603,500 of them). He was instructed to 'take the sum of all the congregation of the children of Israel' and judge which males of 20 years old and more were able to 'go forth to war in Israel'. Thus, Moses became the first known census

The Census at Bethlehem, as portrayed by Pieter Bruegel in 1566.

enumerator. This process of assessing men fit to fight in order to raise an army finds its parallel some 2,500 years later when the need to find troops to fight Napoleon's forces was one of the main justifications for the first British census in 1801.

As one might expect, the Romans did carry out a population survey during their occupation of Britain from the first to the fifth century, but no detailed records have survived. In fact, none do survive until the eleventh century. When William the Conqueror landed in Sussex in 1066, one of his first tasks was to determine how many people lived here, what tax they had paid to his predecessor Edward the Confessor, and how much land he himself owned. In 1085, the order was given to make the assessment. That famous historical resource the *Anglo-Saxon Chronicle* records that the king was staying at Gloucester with his witan (counsellors) and discussing ownership of land and property. He accordingly sent men out into every shire with the task of ascertaining how much land and cattle the king owned

An extract of some of the entries from the *Domesday Book*. William I's wide-ranging survey of his lands was a massive undertaking.

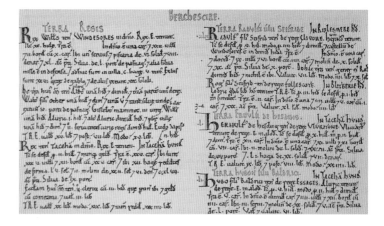

in each hundred (see page 7) and how much revenue each ought to provide. His men were also charged to write down how much land his archbishops, bishops and earls owned.

This great land survey, not known as the *Domesday Book* until some hundred years later (because its irrefutable contents were believed to last until the Day of Judgement), was a massive undertaking, as over 3,400 towns and villages were recorded. Remarkably, the whole work seems to have been copied in the same hand (by just one scribe), over the course of a single year. For assessment purposes the country was divided into seven regions or 'circuits' and in each hundred within the circuit the sheriff, priest, reeve and six villeins swore an oath to disclose who held what. By 1087 the work was finished. However, considerable swathes of England were missing, including Winchester, London and the whole of Northumbria. It is important to remember that this was not a head count; it was land and ownership that the king was interested in. *Little Domesday*, a sort of companion volume, contained details of Essex, Suffolk and Norfolk, even taking account of how many cows, pigs and sheep were to be found in each hundred.

William's motive in compiling this record was not for historical purposes; it was primarily to raise money. He wanted to know who held land in King Edward the Confessor's time

HIDES AND HUNDREDS

In the early medieval period, although no centralised mechanism existed for counting the population of the whole of England, the areas where the people lived were clearly delineated. Counties (or shires, with a 'shire reeve', or sheriff as an official), which we still recognise today, were divided into smaller subdivisions for various administrative and judicial purposes. The largest of these was a hundred, a word of obscure origin, but popularly supposed to refer to a hundred hides. A hide was an ancient unit of land considered sufficient to support one peasant family. This unit is referred to in the tenth-century epic poem *Beowulf*, wherein the eponymous hero is given by Hygelac, King of the Geats, '7,000 hides, hall and throne' as a reward for his courageous deeds, most notably the killing of the monster Grendel.

The parish, first used in the thirteenth century, was a purely ecclesiastical term to denote an area of land with a church at its heart, where the rector or vicar (acting on behalf of the landowner) would collect tithes from those who worked the land within it. Until the Local Government Act of 1894, the hundred was the only unit between a parish and a county, except in Sussex, where groups of hundreds are called 'rapes', and in Kent, where the term 'lathe' was used.

A seventeenth-century map of the rapes of Sussex. Another term to add to this vocabulary of county subdivisions is the 'wapentake'. Originally a Norse term, meaning 'the taking of weapons' and implying a conspicuously warlike culture, it was the equivalent of hundred in English counties within the Danelaw (those north of a line stretching roughly from London to Liverpool) where the laws of the invading Danes prevailed.

The parish chest at St Andrew's, Hoo, Suffolk. Precious parish records would be stored in chests such as this.

(*tempore regis Edwardi*), how much they paid him and, importantly, who could pay more. Furthermore, the money that had previously been raised to pay the Danegeld, the protection money to Nordic invaders, was now to come to him. King Harold, whom he had overcome at the Battle of Hastings, was airbrushed out of the picture altogether in the narrative, despite having been on the throne for 9 months; there is merely the occasional mention of 'eorl Harald'.

At the end of it all, it was revealed that about one fifth of England was owned by the king, one quarter by the Church, and about a half by William's French or Flemish followers who had crossed with him in 1066. The startling conclusion was that the majority of the land was owned by eleven men, out of an estimated population of around 1.7 million.

For all its incompleteness, inaccuracies and failure to state how many people actually lived in post-Conquest England, the *Domesday Book* was an extraordinary achievement unmatched in its scope until the first official census in 1801.

The next significant date in the evolution of the census was 1538, when Thomas Cromwell, Henry VIII's chief minister, instituted parish registers to record births, marriages and deaths. Hitherto this function had been performed by priests in a piecemeal fashion, often recording in the margins of other texts, particularly Bibles, such details of the most important

Baptismal Register for Stratford Parish Church for 1564, showing in Latin the baptism of Shakespeare.

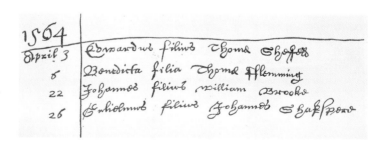

A record of burials due to smallpox from the parish of Dymock, Gloucestershire, 1770s.

families in the neighbourhood; little was formalised. (This same principle of recording family events for posterity existed well into the twentieth century.) Cromwell, in this post-Reformation era, brought a rigour to the process of what we would now term 'data collection'. The registers, of which only about 800 still exist from the earliest period, were kept in a 'sure coffer' with two locks, the key of one being kept by the vicar and the other by the churchwarden.

Few parishes have an unbroken line of registers from 1538; there are many gaps when the Catholic Mary Tudor was on the throne from 1553 to 1558 and also during the Civil War of the 1640s. In 1558 parchment replaced paper and in 1597 each parish produced an extra copy for the Bishop of the diocese. Such duplication was thus a boon for historians.

In the eighteenth century the process was gradually regularised and secularised. A stamp duty of 3 pence on every entry was introduced in 1783, but evasion was so prolific that the duty was repealed in 1794. From 1812, births, marriages and deaths were entered in a specially printed book, and in 1837 Civil Registration was introduced, thereby removing from parishes the task of making and maintaining such records.

MALTHUS AND RICKMAN: FATHERS OF THE CENSUS

Tʜᴏᴍᴀs R. Mᴀʟᴛʜᴜs (1766–1834) was a political economist, statistician and demographer. An important figure in the Enlightenment, he was the author of one of the most significant works on population growth in modern times. In the same year as becoming a curate in the Surrey village of Albury (1798) he published *An Essay on the Principle of Population*. The first chapter of his 'essay', which runs to some 250 pages, sets the premise from which all else follows: 'Population, when unchecked, increases in a geometrical ratio. Subsistence only increases in an arithmetical ratio.'

As he works his way through the 'perpetual struggle for room and food' he concludes that population growth must be checked, either by 'prevention' or by 'calamity' (plague, famine or war), which he saw as necessary measures to maintain a balanced society. This view is sometimes referred to as the Malthusian Catastrophe. It is worth remembering that the Black Death, which was a world-wide pandemic in the mid-fourteenth century and arguably the greatest 'catastrophe' in the history of the modern world, probably halved the population of the British Isles.

He was undeniably an influential figure. Charles Darwin declared in his *Autobiographies* that Malthus's essay helped him to formulate his Theory of Evolution. But to many contemporary thinkers his conclusions about such disasters being necessary to population control were anathema: Coleridge,

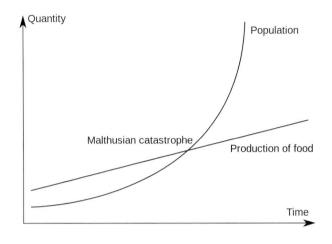

Malthusian catastrophe on a graph, showing arithmetical (straight line) and exponential (curve) increase in population, whereby the population outstrips its resources if unchecked.

who with Wordsworth had just published *Lyrical Ballads*, which beckoned in the Romantic Movement in literature, described him as 'stupid and ignorant'; and William Cobbett, the radical journalist, proclaimed him a 'monster'. These were harsh words about a mild-mannered country parson. But prophets of catastrophe have always had a mixed reception involving scepticism, ridicule and of course fearful acceptance, as we continue to see in some of the twenty-first-century's global concerns.

And so it was that at the turn of the nineteenth century people loved to hate Malthus and his gloomy text, which ran counter to what had been long-accepted biblical truths. The shocking assertions that God would not provide and that going forth and multiplying was not always a good thing to do unsurprisingly upset a lot of people who looked to the Bible to tell them how to conduct their lives. Provoking further ire, Malthus objected to the passing of the Poor Laws, which led to the state's maintenance of the poor in the form of workhouses and other means of sustaining the lives of those at the bottom of the social pyramid. Fear of the workhouse and its degrading conditions became one of the most potent concerns of the Victorian age.

After travelling extensively in Europe and collecting much further information, Malthus recast his views in a second edition of the *Essay* in 1803, and then continued to work on two further editions. He later suggested that the regulation of greed and sexual activity would act as a more acceptable check on population growth.

Although he himself was no advocate of birth control, which he saw as wicked, the Malthusian (later neo-Malthusian) League, formed in 1861, openly advocated birth control through contraception. Concerned at the level of poverty among the British working classes, the League was deemed to be responsible for a significant drop in the birth rate in Britain and abroad, and forms part of the society in Aldous Huxley's *Brave New World*. It was dissolved in 1927.

Malthus is regarded as the founding father of modern demography, but he was also an important economist. He was, for example, the first holder of the post of Professor of Political Economy at the Imperial Service College (later Haileybury School) in Hertfordshire, and his economic theories were reassessed at the start of the twentieth century by J.M. Keynes.

So much for the Malthusian fears and warnings about population growth in the eighteenth century. But what was the population? How many people were living in Britain at the turn of the nineteenth century? The man who set out to answer these questions was John Rickman (1771–1840), a government official, or

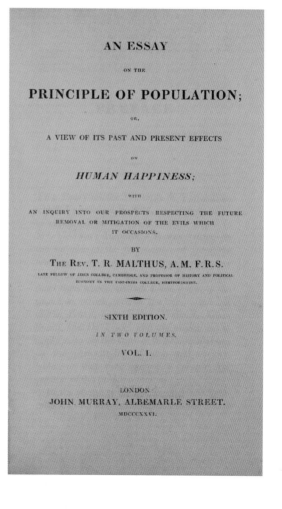

The frontispiece of *An Essay on the Principle of Population* by Malthus.

AN ESSAY

ON THE

PRINCIPLE OF POPULATION;

OR,

A VIEW OF ITS PAST AND PRESENT EFFECTS

ON

HUMAN HAPPINESS;

WITH

AN INQUIRY INTO OUR PROSPECTS RESPECTING THE FUTURE REMOVAL OR MITIGATION OF THE EVILS WHICH IT OCCASIONS.

BY

THE REV. T. R. MALTHUS, A. M. F.R.S.

LATE FELLOW OF JESUS COLLEGE, CAMBRIDGE, AND PROFESSOR OF HISTORY AND POLITICAL ECONOMY IN THE EAST-INDIA COLLEGE, HERTFORDSHIRE.

SIXTH EDITION.

IN TWO VOLUMES.

VOL. I.

LONDON:
JOHN MURRAY, ALBEMARLE STREET.
MDCCCXXVI.

Representatives at the 1925 Birth Control Conference, one of the offshoots of the Malthusian League which sought to control population growth.

career civil servant, as we might say now, who devised the methods to take the first British census in 1801 and prepared reports on the four censuses between then and 1831. Resourceful and hard-working, Rickman showed by back projections how population trends could be ascertained by studying parish records. And in a private paper of 1796 to Charles Abbot, the Speaker, to whom he became assistant, he developed the case for a census, suggesting it would 'offer the government valuable aid to effective military recruitment in the war with France.'

Eventually, by the end of 1800, the Census Bill had been steered onto the statute book, and Rickman was swift to claim responsibility for it. He wrote to his friend the poet Robert Southey:

> At my suggestion they have passed an act of parliament for ascertaining the population of Great Britain, and as a compliment (of course) have proposed me to superintend the execution of it.

MOTHER'S RUIN

To his list of checks on population growth Malthus might have included deaths from gin consumption. The first half of the eighteenth century saw the spread of this new fashion in alcohol on a huge scale. It was believed that gin led to men becoming impotent and women sterile.

Brandy, the spirit of choice among all classes in Britain for centuries, was declining in popularity, partly because of wars with the French. The Dutch spirit 'genever' proved a popular (and cheaper) substitute, particularly when William of Orange succeeded to the throne in 1688. Gin distilleries in London in particular were actively encouraged by the government, which was anxious to prop up grain prices.

The gin consumed was far from the liquor we are familiar with today in a rich variety of botanical varieties; sometimes it was mixed with turpentine or even sulphuric acid. It was certainly lethal, and even given to children in the vain hope that it would nourish (or at any rate quieten) them. Successive government acts to increase the duty were largely ineffectual until 1751 when concern about crime and mortality caused the duty to be increased further, with the result that consumption was eventually curbed. This marks a significant stage in successive governments' concern with public health and their attempts to improve the quality of people's lives.

Gin Lane, William Hogarth's famous engraving showing the perceived evil effects of the drink on the poor.

Portrait of John Rickman (1771–1840), who was the mastermind behind the first British census of 1801 and prepared reports on the four censuses between then and 1831. He died while the preparations for the 1841 Census, the so-called First Modern Census, were in train.

And so it was that the first census was conducted in March 1801. This 'cursory survey', which would not stand up to much scrutiny by later standards, for it was essentially a rough head-count, stated that the population was 10,171,000. Ten years later in 1811 it would rise to 11.9 million, and in 1821 to 14.4 million.

Rickman was no disciple of Malthus. He used the statistical material garnered from his first two censuses to refute many of his opinions. 'The Revd Mr Malthus has assumed there is a constant tendency in all animated nature to increase beyond the nourishment prepared for it. This I consider as a mere and unwarranted imagination.' And a colleague of Rickman's declared Malthus's work 'absurdly mistaken'. Nevertheless, the last two or three years of the eighteenth century set in train much demographic work that enabled the census as we understand it to come into being in 1841, which then went on to chart the great age of British expansion.

LARGE FAMILIES

The popular imagination has always had a tendency to exaggerate the size of families in the nineteenth century, with stories of as many as thirteen children running around agricultural workers' cottages. And even a hundred years ago there was a kind of mythology about large cobble-close families huddled together in terraced houses in industrial towns. Of course, large families did exist, but infant mortality was high. In the churchyard of Cooling Church in Kent the sad sight of thirteen little 18-inch gravestones was the inspiration for Dickens's *Great Expectations*, Pip being the sole survivor of his family. However, statistics paint a truer picture of the size of families. In 1821 John Rickman calculated that every 100 marriages led to 369 baptisms, indicating an average family size of 3.69 children. In 1871, with less pressure on subsistence, William Farr's census calculated that 'children born in wedlock to a marriage are 4.3.' In 1971 it was 2.0 children to each co-habiting couple, and by the turn of the twenty-first century, the figure would reduce to 1.8 children per household.

The thirteen gravestones at Cooling that inspired Dickens's churchyard in *Great Expectations*.

The 1830s saw significant developments in parliamentary legislation, which would have an impact on the way further censuses were conducted. The Poor Law Amendment Act of 1834 was designed to moderate the overall cost of poor relief, making help available largely through the workhouses, entry to which became dependent on a test.

Parishes became organised into Poor Law Unions under elected Boards of Guardians. These unions became the main administrative units for the registration of births, marriages and deaths and then for the decennial census. The Municipal Corporations Act of 1835 led to the creation of new government officials, who would in turn become the Enumerators of the Census. Hitherto, as we have seen, the gathering of this information under Rickman depended upon the often-imperfect parish records.

Following these acts the post of Registrar General was created to head the national system of registration from the General Register Office (GRO), based in the North Wing of Somerset House. Thomas Lister (1800–42), an MP and novelist, was the first holder of this post. Sadly, he only held the position for a short while before his untimely death. Under him the whole country was divided up into registration districts, and a superintendent registrar appointed for each. Further sub-districts were formed, often overseen by the local doctor, who would collect and send information via the registrar and superintendent.

TOWN AND COUNTRY

One of the great shifts of population in Britain over the past 250 years has been from the country to the towns as workforces became required for new industries springing up. The village of Nuneham Courtenay in Oxfordshire is often accepted as the setting for Oliver Goldsmith's poem 'The Deserted Village' (1770), in which the poet laments the movement away from a rural idyll in a village he calls Auburn:

Sweet Auburn! loveliest village of the plain;
Where health and plenty cheered the labouring swain,
Where smiling spring its earliest visit paid,
And parting summer's lingering blooms delayed.

There is little doubt that the poet sees leaving the innocent pleasures of the country for the miseries of the town as unlikely to end well, especially for a homely country girl.

THE

DESERTED VILLAGE,

A

P   O   E   M.

BY DR. GOLDSMITH

The sad historian of the pensive plain.

LONDON:

Printed for W. GRIFFIN, at Garrick's Head, in Catharine-street, Strand.

MDCCLXX.

Title page of 'The Deserted Village' by Oliver Goldsmith, which bewailed the decline of the English village as its population migrated to the towns and cities.

… pinched with cold, and shrinking from the shower,
With heavy heart deplores that luckless hour,
When idly first, ambitious of the town,
She left her wheel and robes of country brown.

Villages had become deserted since the fourteenth century, with the Black Death and changing agricultural methods depleting the workforce. Later, the Industrial Revolution led to the massive expansion of industrial centres. Rickman noted the decline of the agricultural community in his 1821 Census, and the comparable expansion of towns:

Manchester, Glasgow and Paisley, eminent in the Manufacture of Cotton; Birmingham, which relies on the Hardware trade… Leeds eminent for Woollens, Norwich for crapes, and Nottingham for the Manufacture of Stockings.

Gustave Doré, a French visitor, evoked the grim life lived by many in nineteenth-century London in *A Pilgrimage*.

After these are placed the commercial seaports; Liverpool; Bristol with its suburbs...

To take the first of these, Manchester, we can trace through the censuses the extraordinary rate at which the population increased over the nineteenth century:

MANCHESTER'S POPULATION, 1801–1901		
Year	Population	% Increase
1801	328,609	
1811	409,464	24.6
1821	526,230	28.5
1831	700,486	33.1
1841	860,413	22.8
1851	1,037,001	20.5
1861	1,313,550	26.7
1871	1,570,102	21.1
1881	1,866,649	17.4
1891	2,125,318	13.9
1901	2,357,150	10.9

The *Last of England* by Ford Maddox Brown, 1864–6. The uncertainty and resolution depicted in the faces of the couple about to emigrate with their child conveys the spirit of many Victorians seeking a better life elsewhere.

Dubbed Cottonopolis, Manchester was indeed the centre of the cotton industry and by the end of the nineteenth century was the second largest town in England. Young men and women flocked from the surrounding countryside to find employment in cotton mills, which was relatively well paid. Factory owners had invested huge sums in costly machinery, which needed to be kept running, thereby providing constant, if intensive

Manchester Docks in 1883, showing a thriving port and metropolis.

Corby Viaduct on the Newcastle and Carlisle Railway, 1836, by John Wilson Carmichael (1779–1868). Carmichael interestingly contrasts the rural idyll in the foreground with the changing world of industry emerging behind it.

employment. This was in contrast to the more precarious existence of the agricultural labourer, which was more seasonal. Far from the romanticised picture of rural life in Goldsmith's poem and elsewhere, country living was bleak

and harsh. Nevertheless, the countryside did not become wholly 'deserted' during the age of industrialisation. Coal miners, for instance, often lived in isolated villages around a pithead in open countryside.

It was not only the mills and factories themselves that provided employment. These places of work needed to be built and the families that worked there accommodated and fed. Raw materials needed to be transported, first by canals and then by railways. Schools, hospitals and places of leisure and entertainment needed to be provided. The census therefore reflects a massive burgeoning of occupations at this time.

We learn that in the last twenty years of the nineteenth century the number of agricultural workers in England and Wales (including cow keepers, graziers, shepherds, gardeners and nurserymen) fell from 1,200,000 to 870,000, and the number of railway workers rose from 165,000 to 320,500. Similarly, the number of roadworkers rose from 341,000 to 595,000 and mineworkers from 610,000 to 937,000.

A colliery near Seaham, County Durham, 1843, also by Carmichael. Coal was the backbone of the Industrial Revolution and key to the growth of towns, with the mines employing hundreds or thousands of workers.

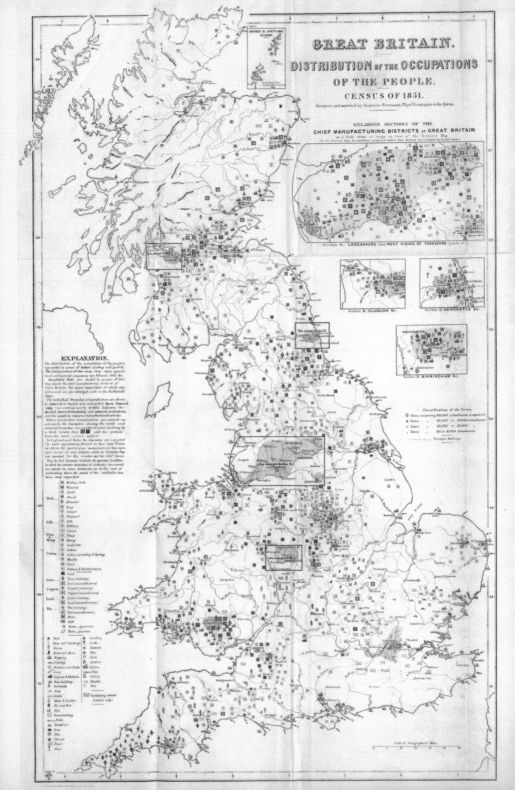

GREAT BRITAIN.

DISTRIBUTION of the OCCUPATIONS

OF THE PEOPLE.

CENSUS OF 1851.

Designed and executed by Augustus Petermann, Phys.l Geographer to the Queen.

ENLARGED SECTIONS OF THE
CHIEF MANUFACTURING DISTRICTS OF GREAT BRITAIN
on a Scale twice as large as that of the General Map
(In the General Map, the portions comprised within these Sections are indicated by border lines.)

Section A. LANCASHIRE AND WEST RIDING OF YORKSHIRE (parts of)

Section B. GLASGOW &c.

Section C. NEWCASTLE &c.

Section D. BIRMINGHAM &c.

ORKNEY & SHETLAND ISLANDS.

EXPLANATION.

This distribution of the occupations of the people is represented by means of letters shewing each symbolic. The characterisation of the map shews alarge spread, hard and pointed occupations are filtered, while the localities that are shaded by means of letters being thus the chief manufacturing districts of Great Britain, the most important of which are delineated on an enlarged scale in the Enlarged Maps.

The individual branches of manufacture are shewn by letters in a shaded type, and symbolic lines between only representing nearly symbolic labourers; the shaded characterisation and mineral productions and the symbolic mineral manufactured articles.

Where particular manufacture are carried on extensively the character shewing the tenth and mineral branches are produced were striking by a thick border, thus ☒ ☒ and the symbolic bear the word (centre added).

In Explanation and Index the character are repeated for each registration District or New Law Union in which the particular manufacture they operate occur in any extent, while in Scotland they are quoted for the counties and the chief towns. They do not, however, indicate the greater localities to which the various branches of industry are carried on, except in some instances as in the case of coalmining where the extent of the coalfields has been duly regarded.

Classification of the Towns

○ Towns containing 100,000 inhabitants & upwards
☐ Towns " 50,001 to 100,000 inhabitants
◇ Towns " 20,000 to 50,000 "
△ Towns " below 20,000 inhabitants
— — — Principal Railways

W.	Woollen Cloth
	Worsted
	Stuff
West		Shawl
	Blanket
	Rug
	Carpet
	Flannel
Silk	S	Silk
	Ribbon
Flax		Linen
Hemp		Thread
	Hemp
	Sailcloth
Cotton	C	Cotton
	Calico (printing & dyeing)
	Muslin
	Lace
	Pottery & Earthenware
Iron		Coal
	Iron (mining)
	Iron (manufacture)
Copper		Copper (mining)
	Copper (manufacture)
Lead		Lead (mining)
	Lead (manufacture)
Tin		Tin (mining)
	Tin (manufacture)
	Wine
	Salt
	Stone - quarries
	Slate - quarries

THE VICTORIAN AGE

FOR THE FIRST time, the survey taken on Sunday 6 June 1841 contained the names of the residents of a particular dwelling and also the ages of those over 15, rounded down to the nearest five years (see page 28). Occupations of individuals were recorded and also whether or not they resided in the same county in which they were born, and whether they had been born in Ireland, Scotland or 'Foreign Parts', as the form quaintly put it.

It recorded information now important to historians, demographers and medical scientists anxious to discover the correlation between longevity and different occupations. It was the first census to be useful for the host of amateur genealogists who now strive to put together a family history (many believing in fact that the census only started in 1841).

As we have seen, the administration of this census was markedly different from the previous four. Inevitably, some were suspicious of the new system with its wider scope and demands for more detailed information. It was feared that the information gained might be used for tightening up on tax collection, or sending the poor back to their place of birth. More generally it was seen as an invasion of privacy and a threat to human rights. As a consequence, some forms were deliberately spoilt (in the time-honoured way of registering a protest on a ballot paper), which caused further problems for the enumerators.

The plight of the hapless Enumerator became a subject for popular entertainment in the later nineteenth century. *Punch*

OPPOSITE
A map compiled from information collected in the 1851 Census, showing the distribution of various occupations, including those linked to wool, cotton and mining.

Taking the Census of a Family, 1854, by Francis William Edmonds.

cartoons illustrated the uncomfortable relationship between officialdom and the working man, whilst in the poem 'The Enumerator's Complaint', published in the satirical magazine *Moonshine* in April 1881, the writer wittily sums up the travails of the Enumerator as he moves from house to house collecting forms. Family historians 140 years later will recognise the difficulties referred to with handwriting, place names, occupations, ages, etc:

The census may be good and right
and useful to the human natur [sic]
But I can swear there's no delight
In being an enumerator;
For up and down six blessed streets,
I've tramped it morning after morning,
And the reception that one meets
Should I serve as a most wholesome morning.

This house, their writing isn't plain;
That house, their language is exotic;
And some describe themselves as sane,
Who seem to me quite idiotic.
Towns such as countess never knew
Are given as the natal places;
While you're supposed to find what's true,
And to correct in faulty cases.
Then ladies of a certain age
Decline to make it clear by telling;

And others fly into a rage,
And oh, such awful slips and spelling!
And some deduce – in humour bold –
Their line from non-existent nations,
And state they've grown uncommon old
In most unheard of occupations.

Here, you perceive that you intrude;
And here, the party's an objector;
And here, they are positively rude –
They fancy you're the tax collector.
So what with humbug and rebuff,
And cutting many fruitless capers,
I have already had enough,
And cry – Confound these census papers!

This census-inspired tea towel of 1881 shows images of the various kinds of people being recorded.

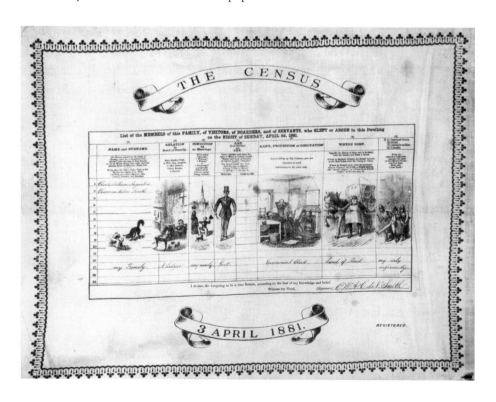

A Victorian wife objects to her husband being listed as 'Head of the Family' while she is described as a 'Female'.

FILLING UP THE CENSUS PAPER.

Wife of his Bosom. "UPON MY WORD, MR. PEEWITT! IS THIS THE WAY YOU FILL UP YOUR CENSUS! SO YOU CALL YOURSELF THE 'HEAD OF THE FAMILY'—DO YOU—AND ME A 'FEMALE!'"

The *Blind Girl* by Edward Millais, 1856. The 1851 Census recorded whether people were blind, deaf or mentally ill.

It is in the nature of all question and answer surveys that the shortcomings and imprecisions only become apparent after the results have been gathered in. For example, the rounding down of adult ages made it difficult to use the census as an accurate source of birth information. Sometimes people just guessed at their ages, for they simply did not know precisely when they were born (birthdays were not invested with the same sort of determined festivity as is the case now); and sensitivities over the matter could mean that a 40-year-old woman might claim to the head of the household to be 39, whereupon the rules would dictate that her birth should be recorded as 35! In addition, those out working during the night of 6 June were left unrecorded, as were those sleeping rough.

Many of these issues were addressed in the great 1851 mid-century census. The exact age of each member of the household was required, with no more rounding down of ages. Each person's

Enumerators often encountered a hostile reception from apprehensive householders.

relationship to the Head of the Household was recorded, as were any members out working at night. For the first time disability was taken into account, with a column to be ticked if any person were a) Deaf and Dumb, b) Blind, c) Lunatic, Imbecile or Idiot. Brutal though these descriptions may be to our modern sensibilities, they were recognised medical conditions to the Victorians.

The intellectual driving force behind the gathering of statistics in the mid-nineteenth century was William Farr, compiler of scientific abstracts and Superintendent of Statistics at the GRO from 1838 until his death in 1880. He was responsible for producing the censuses for 1851, 1861 and 1871. Coming from a medical background, he was interested in using data from the Births, Marriages and Deaths Register to chart the incidences of epidemic diseases and examining the correlation between occupation and premature death. Although he attributed disease to the intake of chemical particles into the blood, rather than subscribing to the biological germ theory, which came later, he nevertheless

OVERLEAF
A census form from 1851, in this case from Bickenhall in Somerset. The pencil strike marks would have been added when the forms were processed.

No. of House-holder's Schedule	Name of Street, Place, or Road, and Name or No. of House	Name and Surname of each Person who abode in the house, on the Night of the 30th March, 1851	Relation to Head of Family	Conditi
Parish or Township of _Birkenhead_		Ecclesiastical District of		
82	"	William Burges	Head	Mar
	"	Eliza Do.	Wife	Mar
	"	Ellen Do.	Daur	
	"	George Do.	Son	
	"	Mary Do.	Daur	
	"	William Do.	Son	
	"	William Wooley	Father in law	M
83	"	Daniel Gange Rogers	Head	Mar
	"			
	"	Harriett Do.	Wife	Mar
	"	James Do.	Son	
	"	Frank Gange Do.	Son	
	"	Charles Albert Do.	Son	
	"	Sarah White	Servant	
	"	Mary Chant	Mother in law	W
			End	
Total of Houses	I 2 U B			Total of Person

gh of	*Town of*		*Village of*	

	Rank, Profession, or Occupation	Where Born	Whether Blind, or Deaf-and-Dumb
	Carpenter	*Somerset West Mylst.*	
		Do. Buckenhall	
		Do. *Do.*	
		Do. *Do.*	
		Do. *Do.*	
		Do. *Do.*	
	Agricultural Labourer	*Do. Bucklands St. Mary*	
	Farmer (Master Farm of 2) employing 10 Men 1 Boy & 1 Woman	*Do. Buckenhall*	
		Do. Taunton	
	Scholar	*Do. Buckenhall*	
		Do. *Do.*	
		Do. *Do.*	
	House Servant	*Do. Staplegrove*	
	Annuitant, Husband formerly China, Glass & Toy Dealer	*Do. Taunton*	
	Parish of Buckenhall		

Hampstead
Smallpox
Hospital, c.1850s.
In this period
more than one
in a thousand
people was blind,
mainly due to
smallpox.

Dr William
Farr, the
epidemiologist and
Superintendent
of Statistics, who
was responsible
for the censuses
of 1851, 1861
and 1871.

had a huge impact on the improvement of public health, particularly during the 1853/4 cholera outbreak in London. He showed that one person in every 979 was blind, largely as a consequence of smallpox, which led to parliamentary legislation making vaccination compulsory. The census had come a long way from being a mere head count of those fit for military service; it was now a vital source of statistics to improve public health.

In some ways, 1851 was an *annus mirabilis* for Great Britain. Victoria had been on the throne for fourteen years and married to the energetic and creative Prince Albert for eleven. There was a very different national mood to the anxious and uncertain times of 1801, when the first census was taken and the country was mired in a war with France. Now, fifty

The Great Exhibition of 1851 was the showcase for industrial Britain, displaying the diversity of wares produced by the British and the Empire.

years on, it was in the ascendant as the dominant colonial power of the world.

This was also the year of the Great Exhibition, set in the magnificent Crystal Palace in Hyde Park. Itself a testament to British engineering and technology, the 1851 Exhibition was a supremely confident expression of Britain's greatness, its central position on the world stage. Writing about her visit to it, Charlotte Brontë, who had travelled by train from Yorkshire,

A handful of the 501,000 British cotton workers recorded in the 1851 Census.

A FAMILY HOUSE THROUGH TIME

From 1841 until the early twentieth century, middle-class families would have had servants living with them. The transcription of an 1851 census return on the opposite page concerns a large seafront house in Lewes Crescent, Brighton, showing us a family of ten being looked after by six servants and a governess, who occupied a strange hinterland somewhere between the family and servants' hall. The word 'scholar' implies no academic distinction, but was used in censuses because until the 1870 Education Act (1872 in Scotland), which made school compulsory from the ages of 5 to 12, there was no compulsion to attend school.

In 1861 the same house records only two servants (when presumably the owners were away on the night the census was taken); in 1871, a family of four with no servants; in 1881 a family of three (that of the local MP) with five servants; in 1891 the same family with three servants; and in 1901 the same family with two servants. By 1931 the house had been divided into five flats, and by 2001, those five flats contained a total of eleven people, and no servants!

This example is a useful starting point for investigations into family history using online census resources. What became of those eight Ravenhill children? And of Fanny Sparkes, their governess? The online availability of census returns from 1841 to 1911 is of inestimable value.

described 'the great compartments filled with railway engines and boilers, with mill machinery in full work, with splendid carriages of all kinds, with harness of every description…'. The technology launched in the Industrial Revolution, as we saw earlier, finds its full expression here.

And so it is that the 1851 Census provides a remarkably vivid picture of mid-nineteenth-century Britain, not just in terms of the size of the population (27.5 million), but in the diversity of employment. Much more detail was asked about people's occupations; for example, Masters in trade and manufacture were required to write 'Master' alongside their

THE RAVENHILL FAMILY, 1851

							Born County	Same County	Foreign Parts
Edward H.	RAVENHILL	Head	Married	44		Vicar of Leominster	Battersea	Surrey	England
Alice H.H.	RAVENHILL	Wife	Married	39	F		Southampton	Hampshire	England
Honoria H. A.	RAVENHILL	Daughter	Unmarried	18	F		Norfolk	Norwich	England
Edward G.K.	RAVENHILL	Son	Unmarried	17	M	Scholar	Norfolk	Norwich	England
Frederick H.H.	RAVENHILL	Son		13	M	Scholar	Littlehampton	Sussex	England
Alfred G.J.	RAVENHILL	Son		12	M	Scholar	Leominster	Sussex	England
Henrietta	RAVENHILL	Daughter		10	F	Scholar	Leominster	Sussex	England
Harvey	RAVENHILL	Son		8	M	Scholar	Leominster	Sussex	England
Cecilia J.A.R	RAVENHILL	Daughter		7	F	Scholar	Leominster	Sussex	England
Edward H.G.	RAVENHILL	Son		5	M	Scholar	Leominster	Sussex	England
Fanny M.	SPARKES	Governess	Unmarried	21	F	Governess	East Wittering	Sussex	England
James	FOOTE	Servant	Unmarried	17	M	Servant	Laughton	Dorset	England
William T.	HOVELL	Servant	Married	30	M	Groom	Edburton	Sussex	England
Mary	HOVELL	Servant	Married	31	F	Cook	Chertsey	Surrey	England
Martha J.	MILES	Servant	Unmarried	28	F	Lady's Maid	Aylesbury	Buckinghamshire	England
Catharine	PARK	Servant	Unmarried	25	F	Housemaid	North Shields	Northumberland	England
Elizabeth	BALLS	Servant	Unmarried	17	F	Under Nurse	Cheltenham	Gloucestershire	England

occupation and to state the number of employees they had working under them.

The total number of occupations identified was 341. We noted in the last chapter how agricultural work declined in the nineteenth century and manufacturing jobs, including mining, increased. Domestic service took up 1.04 million (134,000 males and 905,000 females). This figure increased to 1.23 million by the 1871 Census and then began to decline sharply after the First World War. There were 501,000 cotton workers, 275,000 shoe and boot makers, 268,000 milliners or dressmakers, and 113,000 blacksmiths. There were 75,721 innkeepers and beer shop keepers (which would increase to 94,011 by

Malmesbury marketplace in mid-Victorian times, showing a variety of trade occupations.

1871); and 43,000 commercial clerks (rising to 91,000 in 1871), 37,000 millers, 30,000 horse keepers or grooms, 17,000 hatters, 13,700 staymakers and 10,000 ribbon manufacturers.

Among the professional classes, the civil service, priests, religious teachers and schoolteachers were all around 30,000. Professional photographers boomed from 45 in 1851 to 2,634 in 1861.

The 1851 Census contained an optional section asking about religion; 5 million refused to answer this, as they did when it was asked again in 1861. Of those who did answer, outside Roman Catholic Ireland, most people confessed to being Anglicans, as a kind of easy option. This upset the

Domestic service was one of the biggest employment sectors in Victorian Britain, and was one of the chief occupations for women.

Famine by Rowan Gillespie, at Custom House Quay, Dublin. The work was commissioned by Norma Smurfit in 1997 to commemorate the many people forced to emigrate by the Irish Famine during the nineteenth century.

Nonconformists, who were more committed and precise in stating whether they were Baptists or Methodists, for example, in contrast to the so-called Anglicans, typified in the words of one MP, who on being asked about his religion replied, 'Religion, Sir? I am of no religion; I belong to the Church of England.' It was not until 2001 and 2011 that the question 'What is your religion?' was again asked (see page 60).

THE IRISH POPULATION

One striking revelation of this mid-century census was the sharp decline in the population of Ireland, from 8.2 million in 1841 to 6.6 million a decade later and 4.7 million by 1891. This was due partly to the Great Famine of the late 1840s, when crops, particularly the potato crop, repeatedly

An overcrowded room showing the frequently squalid living conditions of Victorian Britain, c.1850.

THE BRITISH EMPIRE

The words 'wider still and wider' within A.C. Benson's 1902 poem 'Land of Hope and Glory' – famously set to music by Edward Elgar – referred to the expanding British Empire, and this is borne out by census returns. Farr announced after the 1861 Census that while the population of the United Kingdom was 29,321,288 the area of the British Empire was 4,420,600 square miles, with a population of over 174 million. He grandiosely stated:

> It is growing, increasing and multiplying still. And this development of the nation is characteristic of its life… although it cannot be traced to the policy or genius of one man, it will be found to be the deliberate and skilful organisation acting under constant forces regulated by wiser, diviner laws than Plato gave his commonwealth.

The enumerators were able to conclude that India had more clerks per head of population than anywhere else, that England, Scotland and Wales had more lawyers, and Australia and New Zealand more teachers and nurses. All this of course was cited in successive census reports as evidence of British superiority. Urbanisation was marked, with Calcutta, for example, moving from 682,000 in 1891 to 848,00 in 1901.

failed, leading to disease, starvation and death – on a scale of Malthusian proportions. Within five years of the famine starting a million died and (it is estimated) half a million emigrated to America to start a new life, in many cases having moved first to the mainland.

The historian John Ranelagh estimates that of the 8-million population in 1841, half spoke only Gaelic, or else were bilingual. Those 4 million were concentrated in the south-west provinces of Munster and Connaught, the areas most blighted by the potato famine. Elsewhere in Ireland, the population of Mayo decreased by 241 to the square mile in 1841–51, and in Kerry it decreased from 416 to 216. Thus, according to Ranelagh, the famine sadly ended the widespread use of the Irish language. William Donnelly with his 'Social Survey' was the first demographer to count the number of speakers of the native languages. Scottish Gaelic had to wait until 1881 and Welsh until 1891.

As if to mirror the stability of the age, the questions asked in successive nineteenth-century censuses remained virtually unchanged after 1851. In 1861 they were identical. In 1871 the first female enumerator was appointed; according to the Registrar General she 'discharged her duties very efficiently'. Ten years later other women were appointed to carry out the same task. Women's roles diversified from 1870, many being employed as teachers once education became compulsory.

The 1891 Census addressed the consequences of the economic expansion so proudly signalled in earlier enumerations by asking for the number of rooms in a household, in direct response to concerns about overcrowding in cities.

In 1891 over half the population of Wales spoke Welsh.

And Welsh households were asked what language was spoken at home. The findings were that over half the Welsh population of 1,776,405 could still speak Welsh and 505,289 spoke only Welsh. Interestingly Wales did not suffer the same

depletion of population as Ireland and Scotland had suffered, and its population rose proportionately with England's. There was no incursion from elsewhere and in 1851, 88 per cent of the population had been born there. The most significant movement, as had happened in England, had been to the industrial centres of Cardiff and Merthyr Tydfil.

SOMERSET HOUSE AND OTHER HOMES OF RECORDS

Somerset House, that imposing palace between the Strand and the Thames Embankment, where in the winter people now skate in the Georgian Quadrangle, was originally built in 1547 as a home for Edward Seymour, Duke of Somerset. It was rebuilt by Sir William Chambers in 1775 and after various reincarnations as a royal palace and home of learned societies, it eventually became a vortex of bureaucratic officialdom in the Victorian era.

In 1837 the newly appointed Registrar-General of Births, Marriages and Deaths set up his office in the North Wing, forming an association with Somerset House that would last 130 years. There it was that members of the public would go to view the contents of a will or to check the information on a birth or death certificate. In 1977 the Registry moved to St Catherine's House Kingston to become part of the Office for Population Censuses and Surveys, which in 1996 merged with the Central Statistical Office (set up in 1941) to become the Office for National Statistics.

The Public Record Office Act of 1838 had made statutory provision for the care of government records as well as of some privately owned papers. The PRO was based in Chancery Lane (now the King's College London Maugham Library) for 165 years, until 2003, following another Act, when it merged with The Historical Manuscripts Commission to form the National Archives, based at an attractive and spacious site by the Thames at Kew.

The National Archives, where British census records are now stored, are a treasure trove for family historians.

SUFFRAGETTES AND THE WORLD AT WAR

THE FIRST CENSUS of the twentieth century, on 1 April 1901, 'relating to the persons returned as living in England, Wales, Scotland and Ireland at midnight on Sunday 31st March', recorded the population as 41,458,721, of whom 21.4 million were women and 20.1 men. As in all British censuses, women are seen to outlive men. The foreign-born population was recorded at 1.4 per cent, one tenth of what it was to become by 2011. The England and Wales part of the survey records 32 million people and 6 million houses. The whole of the island of Ireland took part in the census, for this was before the division into Eire and Ulster.

The 1911 Census was the first in which the Return was written entirely by the Head of the Household, rather than the information being copied into Enumerators' Books. More detailed information was required, in particular how long a couple had been married, how many children had been born alive and how many had died, and the nationality of any person born in a foreign country. The final column became: INFIRMITY: Totally Deaf and Dumb, Totally Blind, Lunatic, Imbecile, Feeble-minded.

The census continued to reflect the spirit of the age, not just in the questions asked but also in the public's willingness (or reluctance) to answer them. The year 1911 represented the height of the suffragette movement in Britain and increasing numbers of activists would go to any lengths to promote their cause of 'Votes for Women'. The movement had in fact begun

OPPOSITE
Suffragettes
in Manchester
Census Lodge
boycott the
1911 Census.

			HOUSES				Name and Surname of each Person	RELATION to Head of Family	Condition as to Marriage	Age last Birthday		PROFESSION OR OCCUPATION	Employer, Worker, or Own account	If Working at Home	WHERE BORN	(1) Deaf and Dumb (2) Blind (3) Lunatic (4) Imbecile, feeble-minded
No. of Schedule	ROAD, STREET, &c., and No. or NAME of HOUSE									Males	Females					
1	St Michael's Mount (The Castle)						Maud A Lawremore	Serv	S		26	Housemaid Domestic			Devon Callumpton	
							Frances Wilkins	Serv	S		25	Do	Do	Middlesex Hammersmith	
							Louisa Hutchinson	Serv	S		18	Do	Do	London Bow	
							Sarah E Rando	Serv	S		35	Nurse	Do	Lincoln South Kly	
							Annie Brooks	Serv	S		24	Do	Do	Surrey Godalming	
							Ellen Aldridge	Serv	S		19	Do	Do	Bucks Amersham	
							Alice Darley	Serv	S		24	Dairymaid	Do	London Battersea	
2	Do Do	1					Fanny L Dening	Head	S		25	Cook	Do	Hants Southampton	
3	Laundry	1					William G Painter	Head	M	32		Assistant Steward	Worker	Cornwall Gwennap	
							Emily Jane Do	Wife	M		31			Do Redruth	
4	Do Do St Aubyn's Arms	1					Jane Burt	Head	W		79	Licensed Victualler		Do Penzance	
							Honor Do	Daur	S		49	Manageress of Hotel		Do Do	
							Ellen Do	Daur	S		44	Dairy Assistant		Do St Michael's Mount	
5	Do Do	1					Richard Matthews	Head	M	40		Fisherman	Own account	Do Do	
							Christiana Do	Wife	M		33			Do Ludgvan	
							William Do	Son		11				Do St Michael's Mount	
							Christian Do	Daur			9			Do Do	
							Richard Do	Son		7				Do Do	
							Mary Annie Do	Daur			3			Do Do	
							Robert Do	Son		5				Do Do	
6	Do Do The Lodge	1					Thomas John Minter	Head	M	41		House Carpenter at Castle	Worker	Do Ladock	
							Elizabeth A Do	Wife	M		41			Do Marazion	
							Isabella M Do	Daur	S		16	Pupil Teacher B School		Do Do	
							Richard M Do	Son	S	13				Do Do	
7/8	Do Do	1					Jane Matthews	Head	Wid		79	Living on own Means		Do Lizard	
							John William Uren	Head	M	48		Fisherman	Worker	Do St Michael's Mount	
							Lavinia Do	Wife	M		45			Do Manaccan	
							William H Do	Son	S	21		Mason Journeyman	Worker	Do Do	
							Lilian May Do	Daur	S		15			Do Do	
							Arthur Do	Son		12				Do Do	
7	Total of Schedules of Houses and of Tenements with less than Five Rooms	7	1				Total of Males and of Females			10	20				

The 1901 Census return for St Michael's Mount.

as early as 1867, when John Stuart Mill, MP and philosopher, introduced an unsuccessful motion for women's right to vote. Prior to that he and his wife, Harriet Taylor Mill, a passionate women's rights advocate, had co-written 'The Enfranchisement of Women', published in *The Westminster Review* in 1851.

The road to women's suffrage was thus a lengthy one. Emily Wilding Davison, a prominent member of the Women's Social and Political Union, is an enduring name in the annals of women's suffrage. On the night of 2 April 1911, she hid in a cupboard in the chapel of St Mary Undercroft beneath the Palace of Westminster to avoid being entered in the Census. In the event she was listed twice: by her landlady, who assumed she was at home; and by the Palace of Westminster's Clerk of Works, who the following day, adhering strictly to the rule of stating exactly where a person was sleeping on the night of the Census, entered 'House of Commons' on the form.

The 1921 Census again reflected the times: it was delayed for 2 months until 19 June because of industrial unrest in the coal industry, partly due to the lack of jobs for returning soldiers, presaging the general strike of 1926. This was the first census with questions about place of work, the nature of that work and the name of the employer. Perhaps referring to the likelihood of breakdown of marriage in wartime, there was also a question about whether a marriage had been dissolved by divorce. No census at all took place in Ireland this year because of the War of Independence (1919–21), which followed the Irish Civil War.

What was the effect of the First World War on the population as a whole? A rough estimate of casualties suggests that around 700,000 men died between 1914 and 1918, which was about 11.5 per cent of those mobilised. Shocking though this figure

The explanatory notes for the 1911 Census, the first to be filled in directly by the household rather than by an enumerator.

CENSUS
OF
ENGLAND AND WALES,
1911.

[Institution Schedule for Wales with space for 40 names.]

SCHEDULE.

Prepared pursuant to the Census (Great Britain) Act, 1910.

This space to be filled up by the Enumerator.

Number of Registration District
Number of Registration Sub-District
Number of Enumeration District
Name of Chief Resident Officer or person in Charge
Name and Description of Institution
Postal Address

NOTICE.

This Schedule must be filled up and signed by, or on behalf of the Chief Resident Officer or person in charge of the Institution.

The Schedule will be called for on MONDAY, APRIL 3rd, by the appointed Enumerator; in order that he may not be delayed it must be ready with answers written in the proper columns early in the morning of that day.

If the answers are incomplete or inaccurate, the Enumerator may ask any questions necessary to enable him to correct the schedule.

If any person whose duty it is to give information refuses to do so, or wilfully gives false information as to any of the required particulars, he will be liable on conviction to a fine not exceeding FIVE POUNDS.

The Chief Resident Officer or other person responsible is able to deliver the Schedule personally to the Enumerator, or may, instead another person to do so. If desired it may be sent under cover.

The contents of the Schedule will be treated as strictly confidential.

BERNARD MALLET,
Registrar-General.

Approved by the Local Government Board,

JOHN BURNS,
President.

INSTRUCTIONS
For filling up the Columns headed "Profession or Occupation."

COLUMN 10.

1. DESCRIPTION OF PERSONAL OCCUPATION.—Describe the Occupation fully in Column 10. If more than one Occupation is followed, state that by which living is mainly earned.

2. DEALERS, SHOPKEEPERS OR SHOP ASSISTANTS as distinct from MAKERS, PRODUCERS OR REPAIRERS.—All such persons should be so described as to leave no doubt whether they are Dealers or Makers. In many cases "Tailors," "Bootmakers," "Hatters," "Watchmakers," "Goldsmiths," "Silversmiths," "Jewellers," "Chemists," "Bakers," "Seedsmen," "Florists," &c., and their Assistants are not Makers or Producers; in such cases the word "Dealer," "Shopkeeper," or "Shop Assistant" should be added to the occupational name. A person who both makes and deals should be described as "Maker," if chiefly Maker, or "Dealer" if chiefly Dealer.

3. OUT OF WORK.—If out of work or disengaged at the time of the Census, the usual occupation must be stated.

4. THE OCCUPATIONS OF WOMEN engaged in any business or profession, including women regularly engaged in assisting relatives in trade or business, must be fully stated. No entry should be made in the case of wives, daughters, or other female relatives wholly engaged in domestic duties at home.

5. CHILDREN AT SCHOOL AND STUDENTS.—For all persons over ten years of age attending school write "School," and for those attending colleges, evening schools, or other instructional classes, or receiving instruction privately, write "Student." If studying for any profession, state the profession, as "Law Student," "Medical Student." If attending school or other classes half time or part time only, write "School part time," or "Student part time." If also engaged in any employment state the employment, as "School, Newsboy"; "School, Grocer's Errand Boy"; "School part time, Cotton Roving Frame Doffer."

6. RETIRED OR PENSIONED.—If retired or pensioned state the fact, and add former Occupation, as "Retired Farmer," "Retired Butcher," "Police Pensioner," &c. The present occupation, if any, of pensioners should also be stated in all cases, as "Army Pensioner, Bank Porter," &c.

7. PRIVATE MEANS.—For persons neither following nor having followed a profession or occupation, but deriving their income from private sources, or allowances, write "Private Means."

8. VAGUE OR INDEFINITE TERMS MUST NOT BE USED ALONE, such for example as Apprentice, Assistant, Canvasser, Collector, Contractor, Foreman, Inspector, Labourer, Machinist, Manager, Manufacturer, Mechanic, Millhand, Overlooker, Superintendent (see also paragraphs a to v below). Care should be taken that no occupational name common to different industries is used without a full and distinctive description; an Enameller should be described as a "Pottery Enameller," "Watch-dial Enameller," "Cycle Enameller," &c.; a Painter as a "Painter (Artist)," "Ship Painter," "House Painter," &c.; a Riveter, as a "Boiler Riveter," "Ship Plate Riveter," "Boot Riveter," &c.

(a) ARMY, NAVY, CIVIL SERVICE, MUNICIPAL SERVICE, &c. State the service and rank or grade.

(b) CLERGYMAN, PRIEST, MINISTER. State whether "Clergyman (Established Church)," "Roman Catholic Priest," "Wesleyan Methodist Minister," &c. Clergymen who are also Schoolmasters should be returned as Schoolmasters. In the case of Local or Occasional Preachers, the ordinary occupation only should be given.

(c) LEGAL PROFESSION. State whether "Barrister," "Solicitor," "Solicitor's Articled Clerk," "Law Clerk," &c.

(d) AGENT, BROKER, BUYER, MERCHANT, SALESMAN, COMMERCIAL TRAVELLER. State particular kind of business or trade, as "Cycle Agent," "Sugar Broker," "Coal Merchant," "Commercial Traveller, Millinery."

(e) CLERK. State whether "Bank Clerk," "Insurance Clerk," "Law Clerk," "Bookstall Clerk," "Hotel Clerk," "Railway Clerk," "Theatre Clerk," &c.

(f) ENGINEERING AND METAL TRADES. State precise branch of trade and nature of operation, as "Engineer's Pattern Maker," "Ship Fitter's Helper," "Iron Worker" is too indefinite; state whether employed at Blast Furnace, Puddling Furnace, Iron Foundry, &c.

(g) ENGINEMAN, ENGINE DRIVER, STOKER, FIREMAN. State whether "Railway Engine Stoker," "Traction Engine Driver," "Stationary Engineman," "Gas Stoker," "Furnace Stoker at Potteries," &c.

(h) COTTON, WOOL, SILK OR OTHER TEXTILE OPERATIVE, DYER, BLEACHER, &c. State the material and the precise occupation, as "Bobbin Carrier in Cotton Spinning Room," "Silk Throwster's Piecer," "Fluiter in Cotton Finishing Works."

(i) MINER, QUARRYMAN. State kind of mine or quarry, and nature of work, as "Coal Miner, Hewer," "Colliery Horsekeeper (below ground)," "Colliery Lamp Examiner (above ground)," "Colliery Labourer (above ground)," "Copper-ore in Ironstone Mine," "Delver in Stone Quarry," "Rockman in Slate Quarry."

(j) FARMER. State whether "Farmer," "Grazier," or "Farm Bailiff." Farmers' sons or other relatives assisting in the work of the farm should be returned as "Farmer's Son working on Farm," "Farmer's Brother working on Farm," "Farmer's Daughter, Dairy work," &c.

(k) FARM SERVANT. State nature of work, and indicate if mainly in charge of horses, cattle, &c., as "Horseman on Farm," "Waggoner on Farm," "Cowman on Farm," "Shepherd." A Labourer on a Farm whose work is of a general character should be described as "Farm Labourer," not simply as a Labourer.

(l) LABOURER, PORTER, &c. State nature of employment, as "Bricklayer's Labourer," "Dock Labourer," "Railway Contractor's Labourer," "Farm Labourer," "General Labourer," "Coal Porter," "Railway Porter," &c. The terms "Labourer," "Porter," should never be used alone.

(m) DOMESTIC SERVICE. State nature of service, as "Cook (Domestic)," "Housemaid (Domestic)," "Gardener (Domestic)," "Coachman (Domestic)," "Nursery Governess."

(n) SERVANTS, WAITERS, &c., IN HOTELS, CLUBS, RESTAURANTS AND BOARDING HOUSES. State nature of employment and avenue in which engaged, as "Hotel Cook," "Hall Porter at Club," "Hotel Waiter," "Restaurant Waitress."

(o) NURSE. State whether "Nurse (Domestic)," "Monthly Nurse," "Sick Nurse," &c.

(p) GARDENER. State whether "Gardener (Domestic)," "Market Gardener," "Jobbing Gardener," "Nurseryman," &c.

(q) COACHMAN, GROOM, MOTOR-CAR DRIVER. State whether employed in Cab, Omnibus, Domestic, or other service, as "Coachman (Domestic)," "Chauffeur (Domestic)," "Motor-Bus Driver," "Tramway Motor Man."

COLUMN 11.

9. INDUSTRY OR SERVICE WITH WHICH CONNECTED. The information asked for in this column is required in order to ascertain for each industry or service how many persons are employed therein, or in connection therewith; thus, for instance, for breweries it is desired to show how many coopers, blacksmiths, bricklayers, &c. are in the direct employment of the brewery, as well as the numbers actually engaged in brewing processes. Further, it is desired to ascertain the number of persons directly employed by central or local government authorities, whether in administration or in undertakings such as tramways, gasworks, &c. Following are examples of cases in which entries should be made in Column 11 as well as in Column 10.

Column 10. Personal Occupation.	Column 11. Industry or Service with which worker is connected.	Column 10. Personal Occupation.	Column 11. Industry or Service with which worker is connected.	Column 10. Personal Occupation.	Column 11. Industry or Service with which worker is connected.	Column 10. Personal Occupation.	Column 11. Industry or Service with which worker is connected.
Blacksmith's Striker	Slate Quarry	Copper Roller Engraver	Calico Printer	Housekeeper	Drapery Warehouse	Ship Fitter	Harbour Board.
Bricklayer	Blast Furnace.	Cotton Drawing Frame Tenter	Copper Manufacturer.	Iron Founder	General Engineer.	Insurance Company.
Cardboard Box Maker	Soap Manufacture.		Iron.	Iron Moulder	Stove, Grate Maker.	Typefounder	Type Foundry.
Carman	General Carrier.	Tinner	County Council.	Iron Sounder	Govt. Dockyard.	Typefounder	General Printers.
Carter	Railway Company.	Hotel Manager	Railway Company.	Lightwoman	Counter Works.	Wooden Box Maker	Glass Bottle Works.
Carter on Sewage Farm	Urban Dist. Council.	House Painter	Building.	Maltster	Maltster.	Wood Sawyer	Joinery Works.
Clay Miner	Pottery Manufacture.	House Painter	Chemical Manufac.	Maltster's Labourer	Maltster.	Wood Sawyer	Pianoforte Works.
Dual Porter, Gasworks	Borough Council.	Hotel Painter	Hotel Company.	Railway Engine Driver	Brewer.	Wood Sawyer	Rly. Ca.'s Carriage Wks.

(M9627) Wt. 22313—54. 500. 1/11. No. 13.   Harrison & Sons, Printers, St. Martin's Lane, London, W.C.

A plaque on a cupboard door in Westminster commemorates where Suffragette Emily Wilding Davison hid during the 1911 Census.

Casualties in the First World War had a lesser effect on British population figures than might be expected, but many soldiers returned with life-changing injuries that would affect the jobs they could do thereafter.

is, there had been a proportionately greater loss of life in the Crimean War of 1856. There was indeed a decrease in population growth in the 1910s so that by 1921 it stood at 5 per cent after the 10.4 per cent in 1901. This was not so much because so many young Englishmen lay dead on French battlefields but because surviving couples were reluctant to bring new lives into an uncertain world. In fact, the population growth rate, having been in the teens during the nineteenth century, remained in single figures throughout the twentieth century.

In 1921 there were almost 2 million more females in Britain than males. And of those men who did return from the war, large numbers were disabled. From 1911 to 1921 women's employment in all jobs, from agriculture to metalworking and from lodging house keepers to laundry workers, increased. Among the professions, medicine saw a startling increase of 163 per cent, from 477 to 1,253. The number of male doctors remained stationary, at around 22,900.

SPANISH FLU

An even greater killer in 1918–19, and one that was not widely reported at the time for the sake of morale, was the so-called Spanish flu. Originally identified in Spain, neutral during the Great War, it probably originated in the trenches on the Western Front, the unhygienic conditions allowing the airborne virus to spread when immune systems were weak. As soldiers returned home they took the virus with them in trains, through stations and out into the countryside and suburbs. It spread in a series of waves, with young men and women in their twenties and thirties being most at risk. It is estimated that 50 million people worldwide died, including 228,000 in Britain, after a quarter of the population were affected.

The 1931 Census was duly taken on 26 April, and for the first time there was a question about 'usual place of residence'. In one of the great setbacks to demographic studies, the records for England and Wales were destroyed in a fire while in store at the Office of Works at Hayes, Middlesex, in 1942. This had nothing to do with enemy action during the Second World War, and in spite of six paid watchers being present was a 'mystery that will need investigation' – according to a letter published on the National Archives website. Some analysis of the 1931 figures survive, notably a small decrease in the population since 1921 of 0.9 per cent.

One of the analysing machines used to process information from the 1931 Census.

In a reflection of the age it was also the first census to record 'out of work' in its categories of occupation.

A further interruption to the decennial flow of the census came in 1939. Following the declaration of war, The National Registration Act was passed on 5 September. This established a system of identity cards that

A large number of female office workers compile information from the 1931 Census at the Pensions Office (Registrar General's Office) in Acton, London, in July 1932.

THE HOLLERITH MACHINE TABULATOR

Until 1911 most of the collating and analysing of the data collected had been undertaken by an army of clerks with pens and paper, as in John Rickman's and William Farr's day. In 1911 the GRO introduced Hollerith Machine Tabulators, invented in the US in 1890 and soon used throughout Europe. Through a system of spring-loaded pins passing through holes in information cards, an electrical circuit was produced to move the dial of a counter on one position. The bottlenecks that had previously held up the GRO's system of manual data collection were removed and a whole new world of statistical possibilities was opened up. The machines laid the foundations for IBM.

were required to be produced on demand or within 48 hours. The information required was name, age, address, occupation, marital status and membership of forces. The National Register was in fact an instant census, which gave a vital up-to-date picture of who was fit for military service, deemed necessary because the previous census had been more than eight years ago. In 1943 the Blue Identity Card was introduced for adults (prior to that it had been brown, which continued to be used for children). The Identity Card Act was repealed in February 1952; people who had a national identity number during the Second World War or just after still have the same number as their NHS identity today.

ABOVE LEFT One of the identity cards issued after The National Registration Act was passed in September 1939.

ABOVE RIGHT In April 1951 this member of the British Housewives' League burned her identity card and census form outside the House of Commons as part of a protest against man-made food shortages. Non-participation in the census was always an effective form of protest against the establishment.

THE BABY BOOM

National fertility soared in the years immediately following the Second World War: there were 900,000 live births in 1946/47. For some years afterwards, in a phenomenon branded the 'baby boom', christenings continued to outstrip funerals in parish records. A similar peak was reached in 1964; then the rate plunged to 570,000 in 1967 following the Abortion Act.

POST-WORLD WAR CENSUSES

IN THE SECOND decade of the twenty-first century, the *Empire Windrush* (the ship that brought some of the first West Indian immigrants to Britain in 1948) became a potent image of injustice as thousands of immigrants, after decades of living in Britain, were detained or threatened with deportation, being deemed not to have the correct paperwork to justify their being residents.

At the time the pictures of West Indian people walking down the gangplank also came to represent the huge changes that took place in British society in the 25 years following the Second World War, before a series of Acts, culminating in the 1971 Immigration Act, put a brake on the increase, whereby only holders of work permits or people with parents or grandparents born in the UK could gain entry.

Britain joined the European Community in 1973, and the automatic rights that were bestowed on citizens of EU member states had a considerable impact on the demographic. Furthermore, Britain became a refuge for many fleeing unsettled regimes in Kenya and Uganda as holders of British passports. Thus the 'Nationality' question first asked in 1911 now became a much more widespread consideration as immigrants settled not just in London but also in Birmingham, Leicester, Leeds, Bradford and many other northern cities.

OPPOSITE
The *Empire Windrush* arrived in the UK on 21 June 1948.

UK FOREIGN-BORN POPULATION, 1951–2011			
Census	Foreign-born	% increase over previous decade	% of whole population
1951	2,118,600		4.2
1961	2,573,500	21.5	4.9
1971	3,190,300	24.0	5.8
1981	3,429,100	7.5	6.2
1991	3,835,400	11.8	6.7
2001	4,896,600	27.7	8.3
2011	7,993,480	63.0	12.7

Amar Singh, a Sikh, at work on the London Underground, 1964, after winning a fight to be allowed to wear his turban instead of the standard uniform hat.

Another way in which the demographic shape of Britain changed after the war came through the New Towns Act of 1946, which planned new communities throughout south-east England. Crawley, an ancient town between London and Brighton and close to the growing Gatwick airport, was in the first wave of some twenty new towns. Others in the first wave were Harlow and Basildon in Essex and Hatfield and Welwyn Garden City in Hertfordshire. The new towns offered accommodation that was modern, healthy and comfortable, in contrast to older Victorian terraces in the big cities that had been bombed or were otherwise condemned. Census numbers for Crawley, which was to absorb twelve surrounding villages and hamlets, rose exponentially.

CRAWLEY'S POPULATION, 1901–2011	
Census	Population of Crawley
1901	4,433
1921	5,437
1941	7,090
1961	25,550
1981	87,865
2001	99,744
2011	106,597

During this same post-war period the East End of London experienced a decline in population. These census figures for three boroughs show how the population reached a peak in 1901 but then declined after the war. The reasons for this are many, but the bombing, particularly of the Docks, in the

Crawley New Town in the 1960s – a result of massive post-war expansion.

Second World War obviously meant there were fewer homes to live in. Families previously living in Victorian terraces were moved to tower blocks in the East End or to the new towns to the north, south or east.

LONDON'S EAST END POPULATION, 1841–1961					
	1841	1871	1901	1931	1961
Bethnal Green	33,612	74,088	129,680	108,190	47,078
Poplar	31,122	116,370	168,880	155,085	66,604
Tower Hamlets	275,250	489,653	578,143	489,156	195,883

The 1961 Census was the first to contain questions about educational qualifications and immigration. Twelve years after *Empire Windrush*, the government wanted more than a generalised picture of where its passengers were living. In London, West Indians did settle in sub-standard housing and found themselves being charged excessive rents by unscrupulous landlords. Across Britain as a whole, the 15,000 West Indian residents in 1951 rose to 172,000 in 1961.

Under a provision in the 1920 Census Act a mini-census using a 10 per cent sample of the population was conducted on 24 April 1966.

As in the previous century the census form changed very little in 1971 and 1981. The 1991 Census had similar non-participation rates as had happened 80 years earlier with the suffragists' No Vote No Census Movement (see page 45). This time the Poll Tax was the bone of contention. Many believed that the census was a method being used by officialdom to establish exactly who should pay and so absented themselves. Estimations indicate that between 500,000 and 1 million evaded the enumeration. The deeply unpopular Community Charge was succeeded by the less controversial Council Tax, which replaced the flat rate with banded charges, in 1993.

For this census there were also questions about ethnic group, whether the home had central heating, and the term-time address of students. The ONS were anxious that none should slip through the net on census night Sunday 21 April 1991, just as the summer term was beginning. It is worth remembering that overall participation in Higher Education stood at just under 1 million in the early 1990s with the expansion of universities under John Major's government. This figure had doubled by 2016.

Another piece of parliamentary legislation relevant to the census to come into force at this time was the Freedom of Information Act of 2000 (2002 in Scotland).

To mark the launch of the 1966 10 per cent Census, Joan Hunter and June Masson, employees of the Somerset House records office, pose among the record books.

Before this there had been no right of access to government by the general public, merely a limited framework for sharing information. Now any member of the public could access information, whether it related to schools, NHS performance statistics or council expenditure. Those amateur historians who believed that this would enable widespread access to census data after 1911 (when the 100-year rule came into effect) were disappointed. Although there was a five-year hiatus between 2000 and 2005, when access to data was sometimes allowed, the National Archives adhere strictly to the letter of the law, and the 100-year rule is rigorously enforced.

THE TWENTY-FIRST CENTURY

'COUNT ME IN' was the catchy, all-in-it-together strapline of the first census of the new millennium, and 58,789,194 people were indeed counted in. For the first time householders had the opportunity to return the forms by post, rather than have them collected by the Enumerator, and 88 per cent of forms were returned in this way.

Daniel Dorling and Bethan Thomas produced in 2004 *People and Places: A 2001 Census of the UK.* The first report of its kind, it set out to show in over 500 maps and cartograms how life in Britain had changed since the 1991 Census. The authors explained how work and job titles were changing: how many people had found a job after not having one before, retired early, bought cars, gone to university, and bought rather than rented their homes. While many were richer over that last decade of the twentieth century, more were poorer. One of the authors' most interesting cartographic conclusions was that the population was moving steadily and relentlessly southwards.

In order to prepare for this Census, ten factsheets were produced to help each individual navigate their way through the questions and to explain 'why UK plc should count itself in'. These are still available online and between them form an interesting history.

The census form for 2011.

RELIGION IN ENGLAND, WALES AND SCOTLAND, 2001		
Religion	England and Wales % of population	Scotland % of population
Christian	70.89	68.09
Muslim	3	0.84
Hindu	1	0.11
Jedi	0.7	0.27
Sikh	0.6	0.13
Jewish	0.5	0.13
Buddhist	0.3	0.13
Other religions	0.3	0.53
No faith	15	27.55
No answer	7.71	5.49

Individual identity, a sense of belonging to a nation, was more pronounced now than ever before. In 2000 it was declared that respondents in Scotland and Northern Ireland would be able to tick a box describing themselves as Scottish or Irish, an option not available for English respondents, the only other tick box available being 'white-British', 'Irish', or 'other'. However, if 'English' was written in under the 'any other white background', it was not clear whether it would be counted as an ethnic group in the same way as the Welsh. Following criticism, English was included as a tick-box option in the 2011 Census.

As in previous censuses, the questions asked (there were 56 in 2011, with the option of completing online) reflected current social concerns. The Civil Partnership Act had been passed in 2005 and this was the first opportunity for same sex couples to declare that fact on a census form. Immigrants were asked about their date of arrival and how long they intended to stay. Those whose first language was not English were required to say how well they spoke the language. In further recognition of the way living conditions had improved, no longer was the question about access to a bath or shower addressed.

In February 2020, BBC News announced that the 2021 Census could be the last to be carried out. Sir Ian Diamond, the UK's National Statistician, was 'hopeful' that data from

JEDI KNIGHTS

In 2001, the question 'What is your religion?' was introduced for the first time since 1861. This followed the Census (Amendment) Act 2000, which allowed for the question to be asked but the answer to be optional. 70 per cent of those complying in the UK answered Christian, with the greatest preponderance being in Northern Ireland and the Western Isles of Scotland. Christianity was followed by Islam and Hinduism, with over 20 per cent of the population declining to answer the question. These facts are hardly surprising, given the multicultural make-up of Britain in the twenty-first century.

An unexpected statistic, however, was that 390,127 Britons claimed to be affiliated to faith in the Jedi Knights, of *Star Wars* fame, the series of films that began in 1977. People were perhaps egged on to do this by a chain letter that began in New Zealand. This (totally fictional) Order of Knights is depicted as a monastic, academic and militaristic organisation dating back some 25,000 years before the film. For a time this was, on paper at least, the fourth most popular faith in England and Wales. Jedi followers were particularly prolific in Brighton, where they accounted for 2.6 per cent of the population. There can be little doubt that this was more of a protest movement against government intrusion than a considered adoption of a particular faith with only the sketchiest of beliefs.

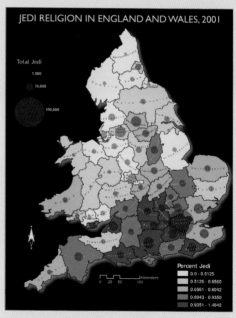

A map showing the distribution of those claiming their religion as 'Jedi' in the 2001 Census.

other sources could replace it. This alludes to a 2018 White Paper in which the government stated that its ambition was that 'other sources of data' would be used after 2021, though it did not explicitly say that the census would be scrapped. The ONS estimated that the cost of the enterprise would be £906m, significantly more than the £482m that was spent in 2011, the £210m spent in 2001, and the £140m in 1991. These costs include work undertaken during the five-year periods either side of the census being taken; thus for the 2021 Census, from 2016 until 2026. Some 35,000 temporary ONS workers were recruited to administer the 2011 Census.

It is worth bearing in mind that when John Rickman came to present to parliament his 'abstract' or report for the first census in 1801 he wrote of the 'terrible inaccuracy of the returns under the Population Act' and how 'only 13 of the surveys from 51 counties were complete'. He in fact gave the impression to his friend Southey that he had managed the whole thing single-handedly.

It is easy to dismiss the earliest attempts to 'count people in' throughout a whole nation of such varied geography and willingness to participate. But how can we be sure in our technological and mechanised age that all have been counted in? Can we be sure that those who sleep rough in cities, those who move regularly from one address to another, quite apart from those who are at the point of death, or birth, are counted on the night of the census? Current estimates of the accuracy of a census stand at around 98 per cent, and perhaps that is as good as it is likely to get with the present system. But it is possible that the National Statistician's 'data from other sources' will prove more reliable. We must wait and see.

Whether or not it continues after 2021, the census has formed a vital part of British national culture over the past 220 years, giving Britons at the start of each decade a vivid snapshot of who, what and where they are.

FAMILY HISTORY AND THE CENSUS

THE NEED TO trace our origins – to discover who our forebears were – became increasingly popular in the twentieth century, particularly after the Second World War, and from the early 1980s the Church of Jesus Christ of Latter-day Saints made the contents of the 1881 Census available on microfiche. The greatest expansion of family genealogy came after 2001, when all those online could examine the 1901 Census so much more readily.

In 2004 BBC Television began the hugely successful series *Who Do You Think You Are?*, with celebrities exploring their past. It both imitates in a public forum what increasing numbers of the population are already doing and encourages viewers to begin their own explorations. In many ways the programme bears out the dictum of the seventeenth-century clergyman Thomas Fuller: 'He that hath no fools, knaves or beggars in his family was born by a flash of lightning.'

The subjects do indeed discover fools and knaves in their ancestry, but also tales of pitiable hardship and oppression and, it must be said, sometimes accounts of outstanding success, for example when ancestral lines to the aristocracy turn up! What is remarkable is the emotional engagement of the programme's subjects as they follow the course of their ancestors' lives. Often they are reduced to tears at the harsh realities of their discoveries, as perhaps is the case with many who undertake their own research.

Nevertheless, the need to discover one's roots, to locate one's precise place in society has been, and will continue to be, a preoccupation of the twenty-first century.

FURTHER READING

Dorling, Daniel, and Bethan Thomas. *People and Places: A 2001 Census Atlas of the UK*. Policy Press, 2004.

Goldsmith, Oliver. *The Deserted Village*. Various editions (first published 1770).

Higgs, Edward. *A Clearer Sense of the Census*. HM Stationery Office, 1996.

Hutchinson, Roger. *The Butcher, The Baker, The Candlestick Maker*. Abacus, 2017.

Malthus, John. *An Essay on the Principles of Population* (first published 1798). Penguin Classics, 2015.

Public Record Office Pocket Guide to Family History. *Using Census Returns*. PRO Publications, 1996.

Also available are Census Reports for England and Wales, Scotland, Ireland and Northern Ireland (London, Edinburgh, Belfast and Dublin, 1801–2011).

PLACES TO VISIT

In addition to the national archives listed below, county record offices contain huge amounts of information for family historians, and such offices may be found in many large cities. Many parish churches also house valuable resources for the historian.

The National Archives, Kew, Richmond TW9 4DU. Telephone: 020 8876 3444. Website: www.nationalarchives.gov.uk (Apart from millions of records, regular exhibitions, helpful staff and reading rooms for research, there is an excellent bookshop on the ground floor.)

The National Archives of Ireland, Bishop Street, Dublin 8, Ireland D08 DF85. Telephone: 353 (0)1 407 2300. Website: www.nationalarchives.ie

National Records of Scotland, 2 Princes Street, Edinburgh EH1 3YY. Telephone: 0131 314 4300. Website: www.nrscotland.gov.uk

The National Library of Wales, Penglais Road, Aberystwyth, Ceredigion SY23 3BU. Telephone: 01970 632 800. Website: www.library.wales

INDEX